Country *Autumn*

Coloring Book for Adults

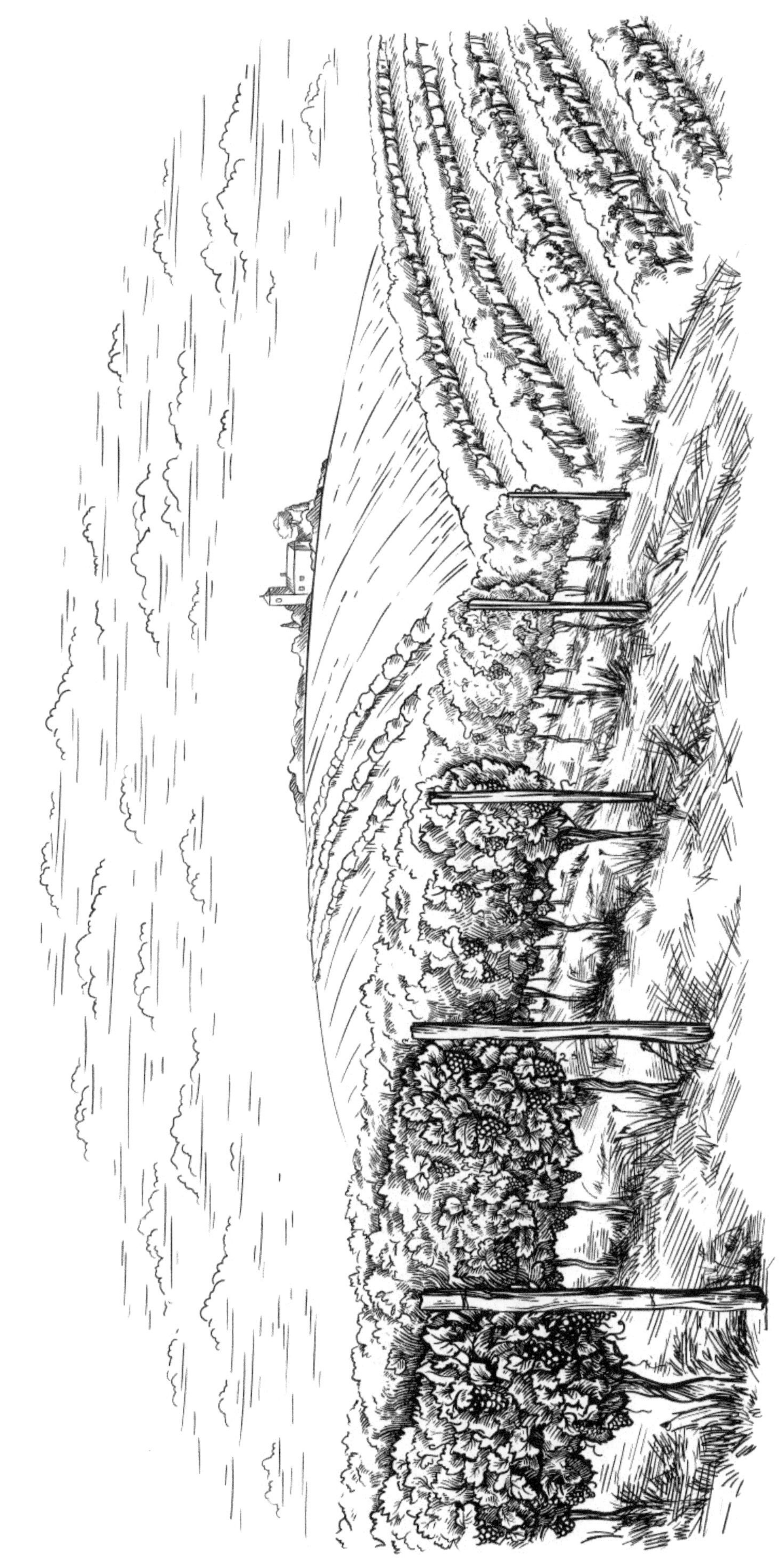

PUMPKIN
PATCH

Happy Thanksgiving Day!

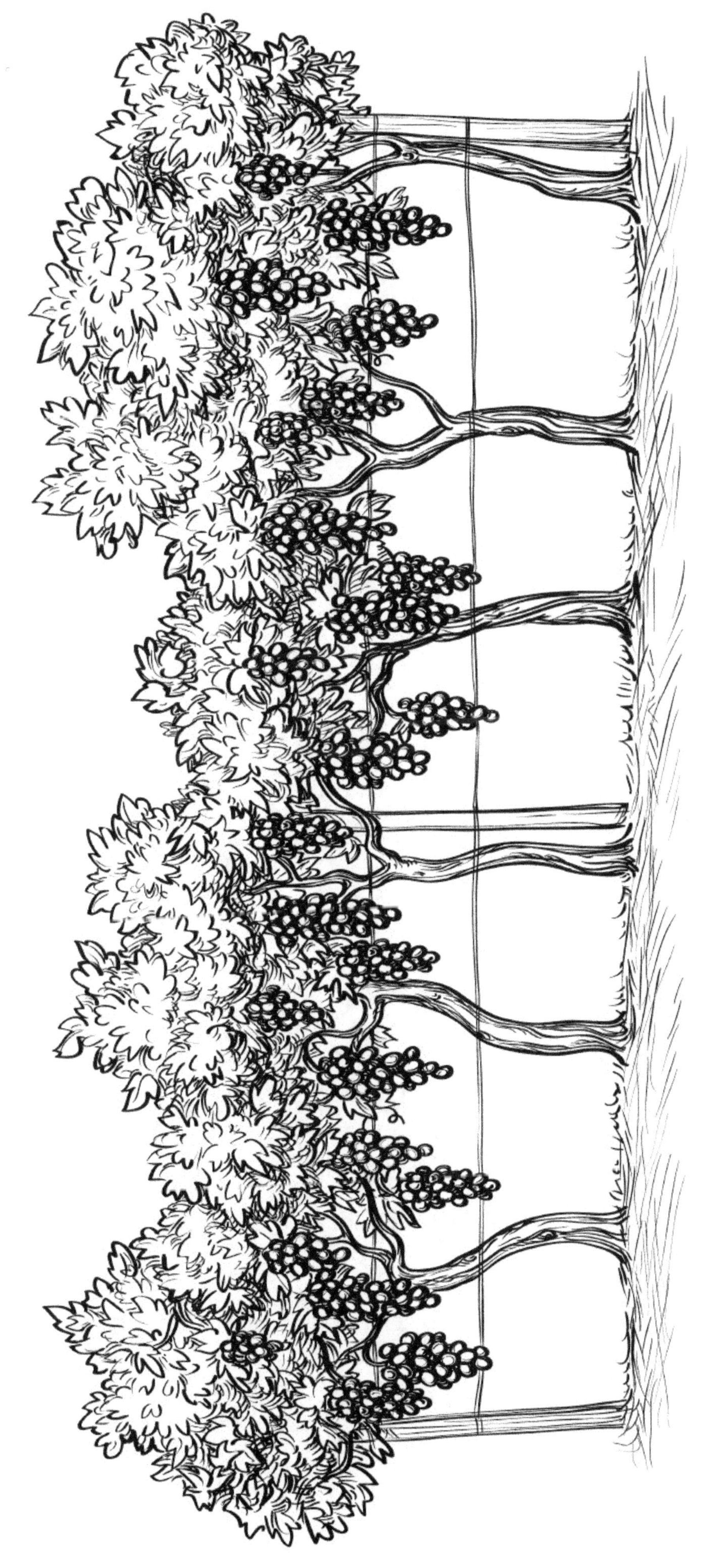

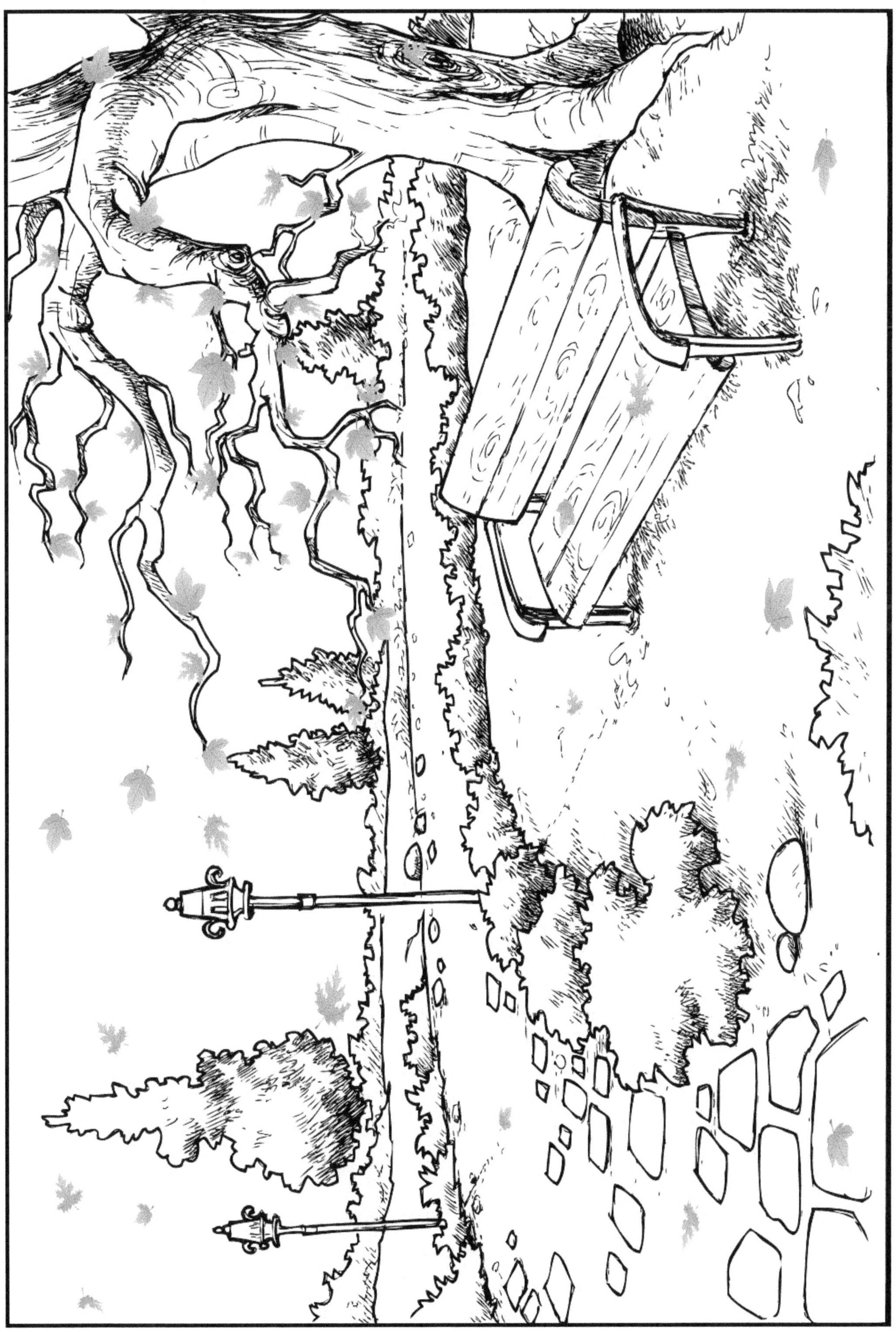

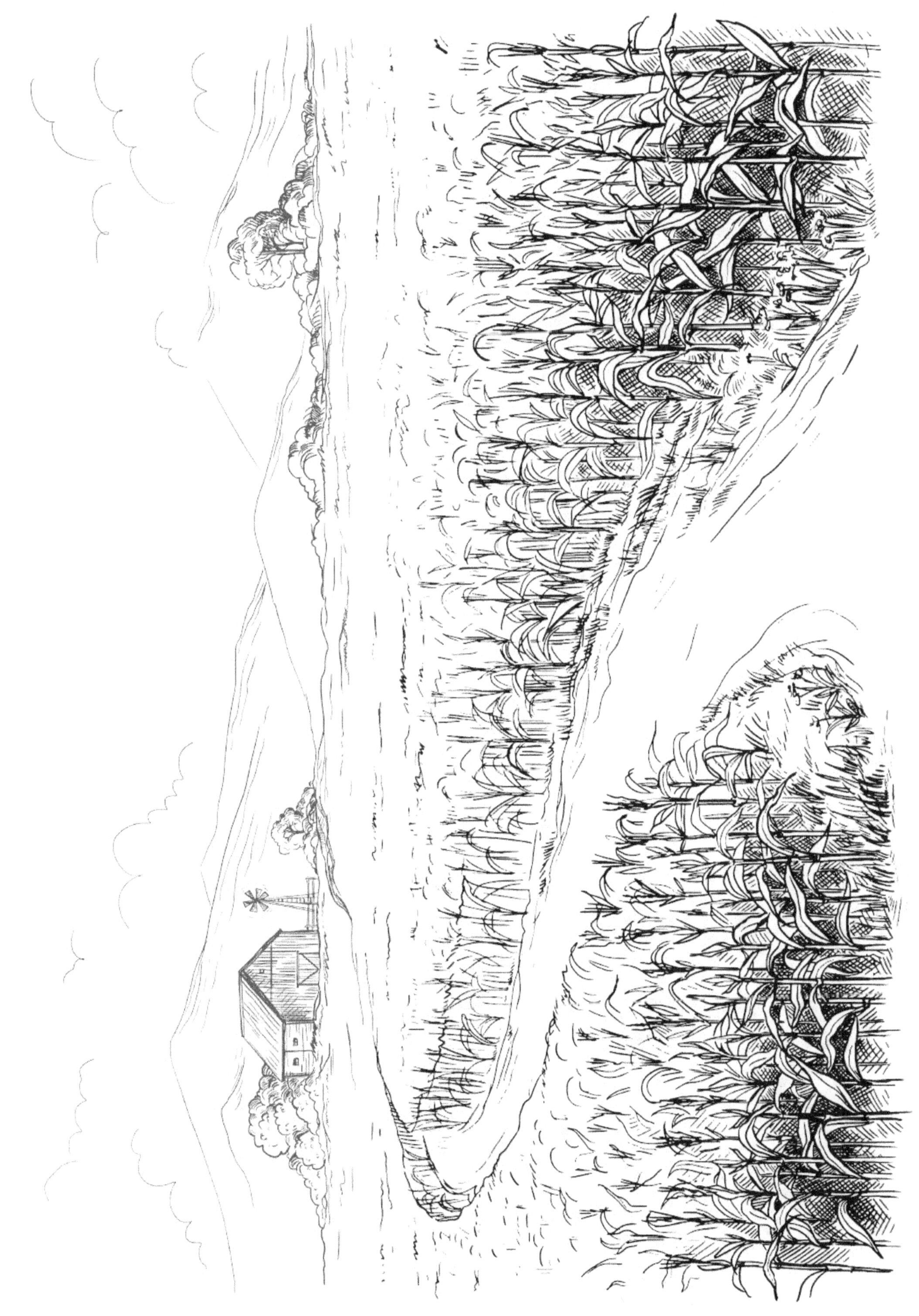

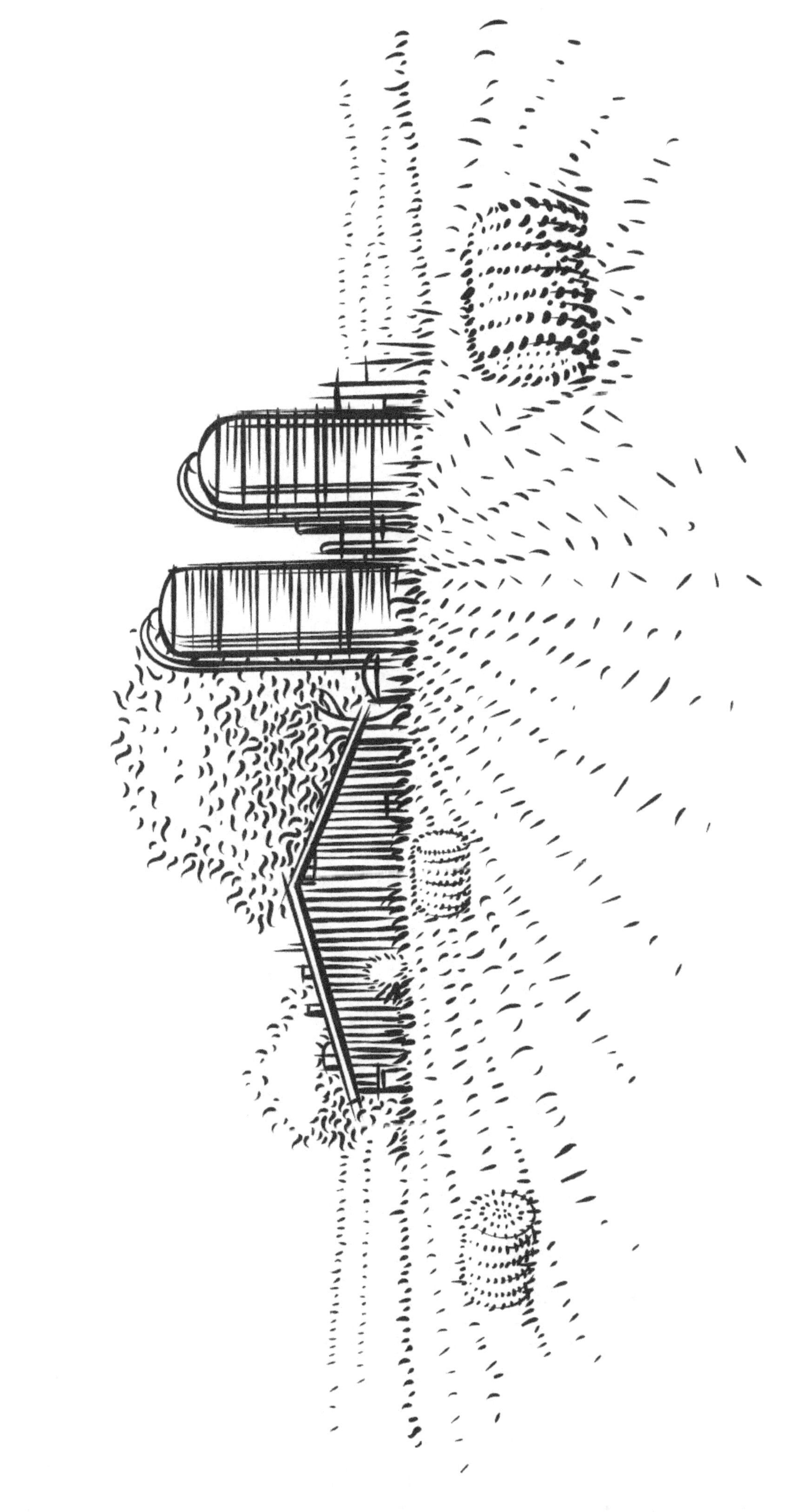

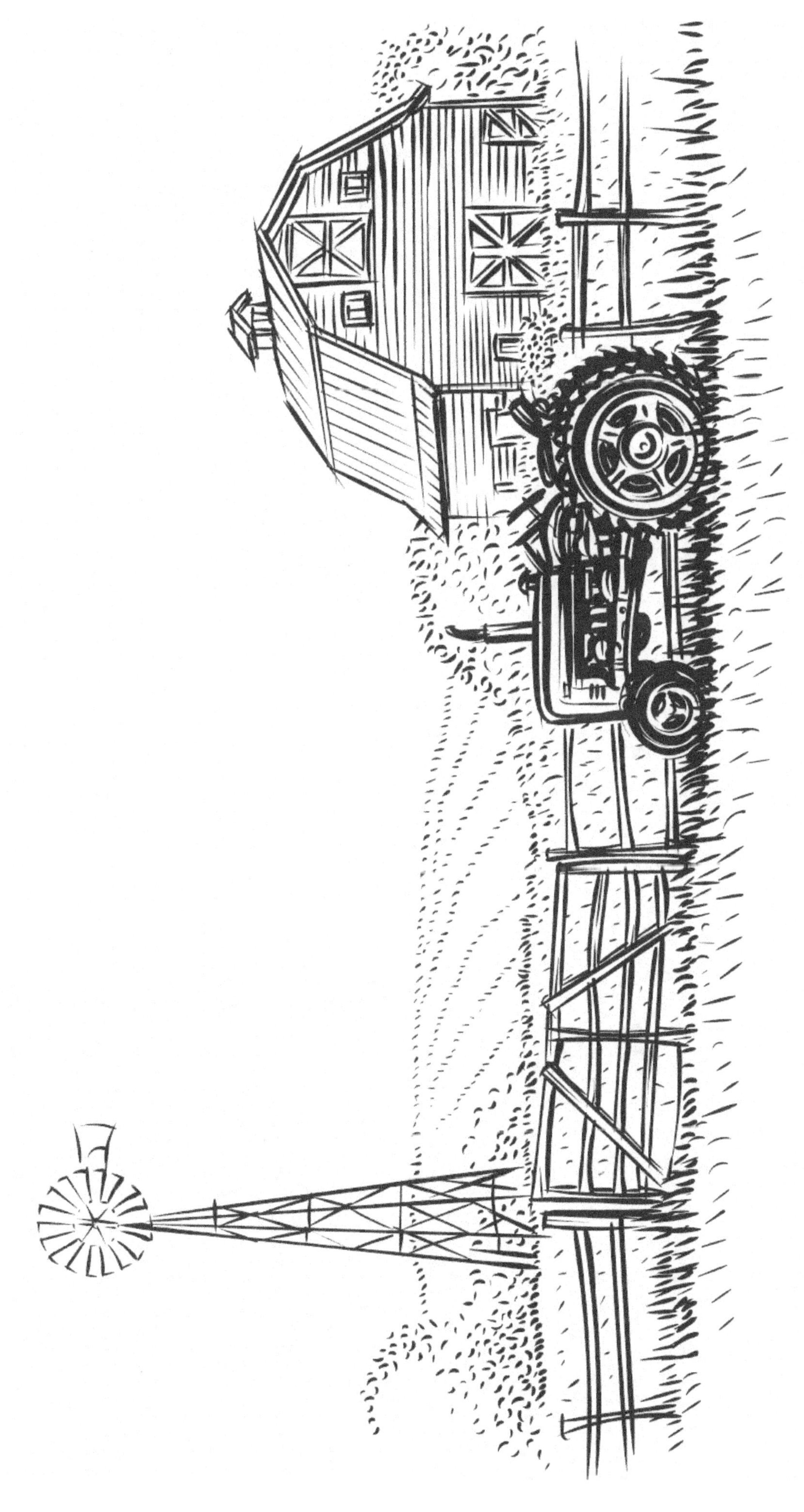

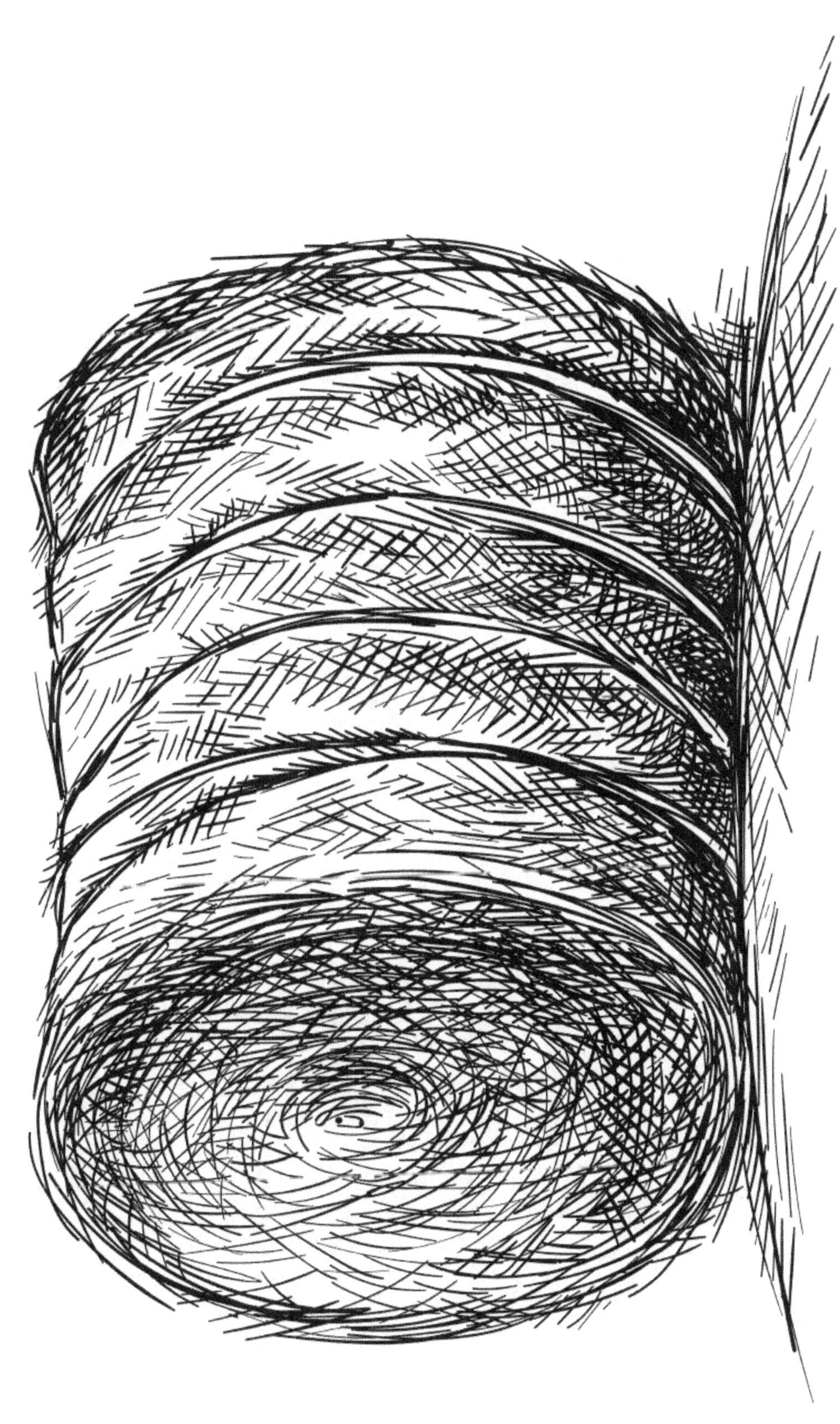

Autumn
memories

AUTUMN MEMORIES